Heard In AA

From Yale to Jail…
From Park Avenue to Park Bench

*A Collection of Inspiration and Wisdom
from Alcoholics Anonymous*

A. G. P.

Heard in AA
From Yale to Jail...
From Park Avenue to Park Bench

Copyright © 2009

Random Bits Publishing
P.O. Box 3662
Santa Barbara, CA 93130-3662
www.randombitspublishing.com
email: randombits4you@aol.com

www.heardinAA.com
email: HeardinAA@aol.com

This book may be reproduced or transmitted
without permission of the publisher.

Printed in the United States of America

ISBN: 978-0-97627-642-5
LCCN: 2008942500

Book Designer: Peri Poloni-Gabriel, Knockout Design
(www.knockoutbooks.com)

Editor: Gail Kearns, To Press and Beyond
(www.topressandbeyond.com)

DEDICATION

This book is dedicated first and foremost
to each and every newcomer in the rooms
of Alcoholics Anonymous.

To the trudgers who give so freely of what they
find and continue to be never-ending
inspiration, mentors and examples on the
Road of Happy Destiny.

To Betty B. who, in my first week in AA, told me:
"You are exactly where you're supposed to be."
Despite my protestations and disbelief, she was
and continues to be accurate.

There Is a Solution

CONTENTS

ACKNOWLEDGMENTS

It is with profound gratitude and appreciation that I wish to acknowledge the love, courage and inspiration of everyone in the rooms of Alcoholics Anonymous. Your willingness to share your experience, strength and hope is reflected in this book.

I'd like to especially thank Cheryl G., Chuck E., Colleen R., Dori O'H., Jim McN., Kathie O., Margie d'E., and Mary McN. for so freely passing on to me the wisdom they have heard in AA.

My gratitude goes to the women at Casa Serena who, on a weekly basis, allow me to witness their transformation and to be of service on their road to recovery. It is a privilege, indeed.

Thank you Joe L. for unselfishly providing the example and support so that many of us can apply the AA slogans and learnings in our lives. Your strength of heart shines brightly.

It is with love and heartfelt appreciation that I acknowledge Leonard C., who steadfastly proved and continues to demonstrate that *no matter what the question, LOVE is the answer*.

Thanks Cory S. for sharing a couple of decades ago that *sobriety delivers what alcohol promised*. I wanted what you had, you kept me coming back, and my family and I discovered that *once you're a cucumber, you'll never be a pickle again!* ✍

With Love and Gratitude,

A. G. P.

INTRODUCTION

For more than twenty years I have been privileged to attend meetings of Alcoholics Anonymous. This book contains a compilation of inspirational, helpful and sometimes downright annoying (it's an honest program) slogans, acronyms, paradoxes and wisdom heard in AA. It is my desire to share this collection of experience, strength and hope with others in Alcoholics Anonymous recovery and with those for whom we may be saving a seat.

Expect a Miracle

SLOGANS

Wisdom Written in Shorthand

> "Slogans saved my life.
> All of them—the dumb ones,
> the imperatives, the shameless,
> witless ones."
>
> —D. CARR

One Day at a Time

Life on Life's Terms

This Too Shall Pass

Expect a Miracle

Just for Today

First Things First

Keep It Simple

Live and Let Live

To Thine Own Self Be True

But for the Grace of God

Think, Think, Think

Easy Does It

Live in the Now

Principles Before Personalities

Let Go and Let God

Keep Coming Back

Let It Begin with Me

Meeting Makers Make It

Mind Your Own Business

Progress Not Perfection

Keep On Trudgin'

Turn It Over

We Are Not Saints

Wherever You Go, There You Are

When All Else Fails, Follow Directions

No Pain, No Gain

You Will Intuitively Know

Some of Us Are Sicker Than Others

Ninety Meetings In Ninety Days

Act As If

Uncover ... Discover ... Discard

Stick with the Winners

Stay Sober for Yourself

Share Your Pain

You Will Be Amazed

Don't Quit Five Minutes Before
the Miracle Happens

Respect the Anonymity of Others

More Will Be Revealed

Count Your Blessings

Let Go of Old Ideas

It's in the Book

You Are Not Alone

Courage to Change

Half-Measures Availed Us Nothing

Happy, Joyous and Free

The Answer to Life Is Learning to Live

It's a Process Not an Event

People ... Places ... Things

The truth Will Set You Free

Into Action

We are Not Saints

You're Exactly Where You're Supposed to Be

**Rarely Have We Seen a Person Fail
Who Has Thoroughly Followed Our Path**

Came to Believe

Don't Believe Everything You Think

PARADOXES

We die to live

From darkness comes light

We suffer to get well

From weakness comes strength

We surrender to win

We give it away to keep it

We forgive to be forgiven

From dependence we found independence

We can best control by letting go

From powerlessness comes empowerment

Keep It Simple

ACRONYMS

AA
Absolute Abstinence
Accountable Actions
Achieve Anything
Altered Attitudes
Altruistic Action
Attitude Adjustment
Avoid Anger
Acknowledge Acceptance

ABC
Acceptance ✦ Belief ✦ Change

ACTION
Any Change Toward Improving One's Nature

ALCOHOLICS
A Life Centered On Helping Others Live In
Complete Sobriety

AFGO

Another F*****g Growth Opportunity

ALE

Alibis ✦ Lies ✦ Excuses

ANGER

A Negative Grudge Endangers Recovery

Any No Good Energy Rising

ASAP

Always Say A Prayer

ASK

Ass Saving Kit

BAR

Beware Alcohol Run

Beware Alcoholic Ruin

BIG BOOK

Believing In God Beats Our Old Knowledge

BTB

Back To Basics

BUT
Being Unconvinced Totally

CALM
Can Anger Leave Me

CARE
Comforting and Reassuring Each Other

CHANGE
Choosing Honesty Allows New Growth Everyday

CIA
Catholic Irish Alcoholic

CHIPS
Clean Happy Individuals Praising Sobriety

CLEAN
Completely Leaving Every Addiction Now

CRAP
Carry Resentments Against People

DEAD
Drinking Ends All Dreams
Drinking Everything And Driving

DENIAL
Don't Even Notice I'm Lying
Don't Even Notice It's a Lie

DETACH
Don't Even Think About Changing Him/Her

DUES
Desperately Using Everything [but] Sobriety

DUMP
Dwelling Upon My Problems

EGO
Easing God Out
Edging God Out

FACE
Fear ✦ Attachment ✦ Control ✦ Entitlement

FAILURE
Fearful ✦ Arrogant ✦ Insecure ✦ Lonely ✦
Uncertain ✦ Resentful ✦ Empty

FAITH
Fabulous Adventure In Trusting Him
Facing An Inner Truth Heals

Finding Answers In The Higher Power
For An Instant Trust Him
Fear And Insecurity? Trust Him!
Father And I Trying Hard

FEAR

Face Everything And Recover
Failure Expected And Received
False Evidence Appearing Real
False Expectations Appearing Real
Feelings Every Alcoholic Rejects
Fighting Ego Against Reality
Forget Everything And Run
Forgetting Everything [is] All Right
Frantic Effort [to] Appear Real
Frantic Efforts [to] Appear Recovered
F*** Everything And Run

FINE

Faithful ✦ Involved ✦ Knowledgeable ✦ Experienced
Feeling Insecure ✦ Neurotic ✦ [and] ✦ Emotional
Feeling Insecure ✦ Numb ✦ [and] ✦ Empty
Frantic ✦ Insane ✦ Nuts ✦ Egotistical
Freaked out ✦ Insecure ✦ Neurotic ✦ Emotional

FINE *continued*

Frustrated ✦ Insecure ✦ Neurotic ✦ Egotistical
Fed Up ✦ Insecure ✦ Neurotic ✦ [and] ✦ Emotional

FIT

Faith ✦ Intuition ✦ Trust

FOG

Fear Of God

FROG

Forever Relying On God

GIFT

God Is Forever There

GIFTS

Getting It from the Steps

GOD

Go On Dreaming
Good Orderly Direction
Group Of Drunks

GOYA

Get Off Your Ass

GUT
God's Undeniable Truths

HALT
Happy ✦ Appreciative ✦ Lovable ✦ Teachable
Hope ✦ Acceptance ✦ Love ✦ Tolerance
Horny ✦ Arrogant ✦ Lazy ✦ Tragic
Hungry ✦ Angry ✦ Lonely ✦ Tired

HALTS
Hungry ✦ Angry ✦ Lonely ✦ Tired ✦ Stupid

HEART
Healing, Enjoying and Recovering Together

HELP
His/Her Ever Loving Presence
Hope ✦ Encouragement ✦ Love ✦ Patience

HJF
Happy ✦ Joyous ✦ Free

HOPE
Hang On, Peace Exists
Happy Our Program Exists
Hearing Other People's Experience

HOW
Honest ✦ Open ✦ Willing
Honesty ✦ Openness ✦ Willingness

HP
Higher Power
Holy Presence

ISM
I ✦ Self ✦ Me
Incredible Short Memory
Incredible Spiritual Moment
I Sabotage Myself
I Sponsor Myself
InSide Me

KISS
Keep It Serenely Simple
Keeping It Simple Spiritually
Keep It Simple, Stupid
Keep It Simple, Sweetheart

LET GO
Leave Everything To God, Okay?

LIFE
Living in Faith Everyday

LOVE
Letting Go of Virtually Everything
Living Our Victories Everyday

LTSM
Like to Sabotage Myself

MYOB
Mind Your Own Business

NEW
Nothing Else Worked

NOW
No Other Way

NUTS
Not Using the Steps

OUR
Openly Using Recovery

PACE
Positive Attitudes Change Everything

PAID
Pitiful And Incomprehensible Demoralization

PAIN
Pause And Invite New

PHD
Pretty Heavy Drinker

PIP
Pride ✦ Impatience ✦ Projection

PMS
Poor Me Syndrome
Pour More Scotch

PRIDE
Personal Recovery Involves Defeating Ego

PROGRAM
People Relying On God Relaying A Message

RELAPSE
Recovery Exits Life And Program Seems Empty
Reliving Every Low And Pitiful Scene Exactly

RELATIONSHIP
Real Exciting Love Affair Turns Into Outrageous
Nightmare ✦ Sobriety Hangs in Peril

RID
Restless ✦ Irritable ✦ Discontented

SASTO
Some Are Sicker Than Others

SLIP
Sobriety Loses Its Priority
Stupid Little Idiotic Plan

SOBER
Son Of a Bitch Everything is Real
Staying Off Booze Enjoying Recovery

SOBRIETY
Stay Off Booze Recovery Is Everything To You

SOLUTIONS
Saving Our Lives Using The Inventory Of
Needed Steps

SPONSOR
Sober Person Offering Newcomers Suggestions
On Recovery

STAR
Start Talking About Recovery

STEPS
Solutions To Every Problem Sober
Solutions To Every Problem [in] Sobriety

STOP
Sicker Than Other People

TEAM
Together Everyone Achieves More

TGIF
Thank God I'm Forgiven

THINK
Thoughtful ✦ Honest ✦ Intelligent ✦ Necessary ✦ K

TIME
Things I Must Earn
This I Must Earn
This Is My Education

TLC
Total Life Change

TRUST
Try Relying Upon Step Three
Try Relying Upon Steps [and] Traditions

WASP
Worry ✦ Anger ✦ Self-Pity

WILLING
When I L[L]ive ✦ I need God

WISDOM
Went Into Self [and] Discovered Our Motive

WORK
What Our Recovery Knows

WORRY
Wrong Or Right Remain Yourself

YANA
You Are Not Alone

YET
You Are Eligible Too
You'll End [up] There

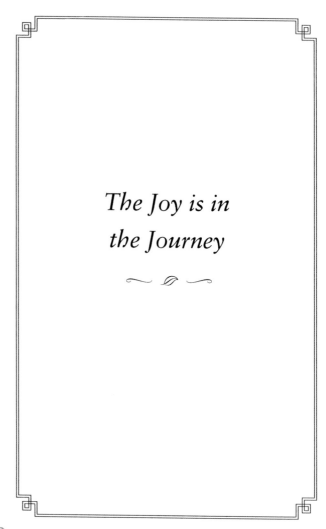

*The Joy is in
the Journey*

INSPIRATION TO AND FROM
THE JOURNEY

AA

I came to AA for my drinking and stayed for my thinking.

AA has a wrench for every nut.

Everything in AA is designed to help me.

AA does not stand for Alcoholic Analysis.

Drinking kills your pain. AA cures your pain.

Nobody can compel us. Nobody can expel us.

AA will teach you to be "happy, joyous and free."

Alcohol took me to my knees. AA picked me up.

AA is a *we* program. I get drunk, *we* stay sober.

Acceptance

- is the answer to all my problems today.

- is knowing the past will never get better.

- does not necessarily mean approval.

You're exactly where you're supposed to be.

Keep your acceptance level high and your expectation level low.

The secret to acceptance is not in getting what you want, but in wanting what you get.

Life is 10% what you make it and 90% how to take it.

Accept. Don't expect.

Page 449 (or page (417) of the Big Book.

Accept the Things We Cannot Change

Accepting what you cannot change takes spiritual maturity and courage.

Things aren't necessarily going wrong just because they're not going my way.

Act As If

It's easier to act your way into a new way of thinking than to think your way into a new way of acting.

Action alleviates anxiety.

Utilize don't analyze.

Addiction

I'm not responsible for my addiction, but I am responsible for my recovery.

Alcohol

- ✍ gave me the wings of an eagle and then it took away the sky.

- ✍ went from being my best friend to being my worst enemy.

- ✍ is cunning, baffling, powerful and very patient.

Most things can be preserved in alcohol. Dignity, however, is not one of them.

Booze did not give me courage. It took away my inhibitions.

Alcohol educates you beyond belief. You get your PHD—Poor Helpless Drunk.

Alcohol's Promises—jail, insanity or death.

Alcoholic(s)

- an egomaniac with an inferiority complex.

- think they are terminally unique.

- are lifelong loners who can't stand to be alone.

- have trouble with only three things: success, failure and the obvious.

If you think you're an alcoholic you probably are.

If you have to control your drinking, it must be out of control.

If you're not an alcoholic, you're not wondering if you are one.

I drank when I wanted to, didn't want to, and any other time.

We drank when it went good. We drank more when it went bad.

We are one drink away from a drunk.

It's the first drink that gets us drunk.

My best thinking got me drunk.

I didn't get in trouble every time I drank, but every time I drank and I got in trouble, I was drunk.

Alcoholic Drinking—impulsive, compulsive, repulsive.

My worst day sober is better than my best day drunk.

My best friend (alcohol) became my worst enemy.

An alcoholic alone is in bad company.

Allergic to alcohol, I break out in spots like Cleveland.

Allergic to alcohol, I break out in handcuffs.

An alcoholic wants to be held while isolating.

I may not be much, but it's all I think about.

If I could drink like a normal drinker, I'd drink all the time.

Outside I was a roaring tiger; inside I was a jellyfish.

Alcoholic(s) *continued*

Once an alcoholic, always an alcoholic.

The alcoholic's favorite brand is MORE.

We may not have had the happiest childhoods, but we certainly have had the longest.

It's an alcoholic's destiny to be locked up, covered up or sobered up.

You can carry the message but not the alcoholic.

We are afraid to live and afraid to die.

Many of us end up job-less, car-less, home-less.

An alcoholic can be in the gutter yet still look down on other people.

An alcoholic is not a bad person becoming good, but a sick person getting well.

The definition of an alcoholic: an egomaniac with an inferiority complex.

You can always tell an alcoholic, but you can't tell him/her much.

Some people drink normally, and I normally drink.

An alcoholic's mind is like a bad neighborhood— don't go there alone.

One drink is too many, a hundred drinks aren't enough.

One drink away from a drunk, and a drunk away from a drink.

Talking to a drunk is like dribbling a football.

First you were funny. But then you weren't.

Alcoholics are just like other people, only more so.

He drinks and he breaks out in orange jumpsuits.

Never went to jail. But when I drank, I sentenced myself to hard time.

Alcoholics are the only people who can feel superior and inferior at the same time.

I suffered from terminal rightness.

Four reasons I can't be an alcoholic—too healthy, too wealthy, too young or too smart.

If you're thinking of your next drink before you have finished your current drink, you are probably an alcoholic.

Alcoholic—under the influence, under a bridge, under arrest.

Alcoholics Anonymous (The Program)

- is a self help program but you can't do it by yourself.

- is a simple program for complicated people.

- is not for people who want it or for people who need it; it is for people who do it.

- spoils your drinking.

- is an education without graduation.

- is a program of action.

- is a lifestyle not a turnstile.

The only requirement for membership is a desire to quit drinking.

The program of Alcoholics Anonymous is foolproof. This fool is proof.

The program of Alcoholics Anonymous is a package deal, but you only get it one day at a time.

It's the easier, softer way.

It's a way out and up.

We may not have it all together, but together we have it all.

If all I got was sobriety, I would have been shortchanged.

The program works if you work it.

Unity, Recovery, Service.

It (Alcoholics Anonymous) works.

Principles before personalities.

With a stomach full of AA you won't have room for a beer.

A belly full of booze and a head full of AA don't mix.

What you hear here, let it stay here.

It's a "we" program.

"We" can do what I can't.

The things we have in common are more important than our differences.

There are none too dumb for the AA program, but many are too smart.

The willingness to be uncomfortable leads to being comfortable.

We don't come to AA because we can't drink. We come to AA because we can drink.

Try it for ninety days. If you don't like it, we'll gladly refund your misery.

It's a selfish program.

Come until you want to be here.

Attendance is not a sentence, it is a reprieve.

We won't keep you from going to hell, nor do we have the ticket to heaven. But we'll keep you sober long enough for you to make up your mind which way you want to go.

There are no big deals in AA. Life has its ups and downs.

I thought I was special and different from anyone else in the room.

It's a spiritual program of action coming from love.

It's not a program for sissies.

Before I came to the program I read a lot of self-help books; then I discovered I had no self.

If you want friends, join the Army. If you want to get sober, join AA.

The AA program is a bridge back to life.

May I never have an original thought.

It's a program of action and change.

I am the black sheep of the family. I came to AA and found the rest of the herd.

Focus on the program, not the problem.

If you're at the center of AA, you can't fall off.

An alcoholic's mind is like a bad neighborhood— don't go there alone.

I'm just another bozo on the bus.

I worked the program until it worked me.

Keep coming back. It works if you work it. Work it, you're worth it.

We're here for a reason, not for a season.

None of us came here on a winning streak.

Out of self and into you (the group).

Out of self and into you—the group effect.

You must be present to win.

When you're at a meeting, your disease is doing push-ups in the parking lot.

We'll love you until you learn to love yourself.

I was going to drink or grow.

If you want to drink, that is your business. If you want to quit and can't, that is AA's business.

You don't have to love the people in AA, but you have to love the AA in the people.

AA is like a lifeboat. I will help you get in but you cannot have my seat.

AA offers hope for the helpless and help for the hopeless.

Either you carry the message or you will become the message.

I did not get here because I saw the light. I came here because I had nowhere else to go.

Nobody is too dumb for this program, but there are a lot of people who are too smart.

The program of Alcoholics Anonymous is a journey from the head to the heart.

When he came to AA, he was a "rebel without a clue."

The quality of my problems is getting better the longer I stay in the program of AA.

You don't get better and then work the program. You work the program to get better.

AA works because it is shared vulnerability.

The saddest stories in AA are the ones we never hear.

To old-timers in AA, being dually addicted meant shots and beers.

If your program is not working, try ours.

In AA we comfort the disturbed and disturb the comfortable.

How to work your AA program: Faith and Footwork.

Rehab is the discovery. The Program is the recovery.

Alcoholism

- is incurable, progressive, fatal.
- is a three-fold disease: spiritual, mental, physical.
- is a physical compulsion with a mental obsession.
- is a self-diagnosed disease.
- is an equal opportunity destroyer.

- is a spiritual malady.

- is but a symptom.

- is cunning, baffling, and powerful; and very patient.

- is like an elevator: you can get off at any floor.

- is the only disease that tells you don't have it.

- is an equal opportunity disease.

- doesn't come in bottles, it comes in people.

- is an "ism" not a "wasm."

- is the "I know" disease.

- is not a moral issue.

One drink is too many and a thousand is not enough.

Alcoholism is a family sport. Everyone gets to play.

For some, it's a two-fold disease: more and right now.

It's a disease that tells us we don't have a disease.

Some of us are sicker than others.

If the cure works, chances are you have the disease.

Incomprehensible demoralization.

Guilt of yesterday, fear of tomorrow, shame of today.

The disease progresses even when you're not drinking.

I was in a black hole without a light.

When you dance with a gorilla, it's the gorilla who decides when to stop.

The man takes the drink. The drink takes a drink. The drink takes the man.

Alcoholism is a disease, not a disgrace.

Remember, alcoholism is cunning, baffling, powerful and patient. "Remember" is the most important word in that sentence.

Alcoholism is a universal solvent. It obliterates everything.

Your disease will come to you like a lover, not a fighter.

Alcoholism is a disease of the ups—throw ups, lock ups, sober ups.

I took a 6-pack into the woods when I was 14-years-old, and I came out when I was 40.

Anger

Fear in a party dress.

Who angers you, conquers you.

Justifiable anger is best left to those able to handle it.

Just put a "d" in front of anger, and you get "danger."

Anniversary/Birthday

Every anniversary is a victory for all of us.

It takes a year to get a year.

It takes five years to get all your marbles back. Then it takes five years to learn how to play with them. And don't pick up more marbles than you had.

The years were easy but the days were hard.

What you want is an anniversary date that doesn't move.

Attitude

Good morning, God. Or, Good God, it's morning?

Attitude of gratitude.

Back to Basics

You don't have to go back to basics if you never leave them.

Beginners

I was a mumbling, crumbling, bumbling, stumbling drunk when I came in.

Beginners who make meetings become old-timers. Old-timers who don't make meetings become beginners.

Even though you don't know it, your first meeting day is the best day of your life.

At my first meeting, the only sign on the wall that I recognized was the exit sign.

I finally found out it was not about stopping drinking. It was about staying stopped.

Beyond Your Wildest Dreams

In sobriety, your wildest dreams may/will come to fruition. Dream Big!

When I came to AA, I was told "things would be beyond my wildest dreams." What actually happened was that my wildest dreams changed.

Big Book

The *Big Book* is your road map; the meetings are your filling stations.

You may be the only copy of the *Big Book* people ever see.

Don't read the *Big Book* like a novel. Read it like an owner's manual.

The *Big Book* is the Bible in drunk language.

Don't quote the *Big Book* unless you have read it.

Bondage of Self

I'm not much, but I'm all I think about.

(Alcoholic) **Bottom**

When things get worse faster than you can lower your standards.

The longer I'm in the program, the lower my bottom gets.

My marriage began with wine and roses and ended up like Virginia Wolf.

When you decided to stop digging.

I hope my bottom doesn't have a basement.

When I first came around, I did not have a license, a car or a life.

But for the Grace of God

Nothing happens in God's world by mistake.

The will of God will never take you where the grace of God will not protect you.

Change

If you keep doing what you've always done, you'll get what you always got.

Change the things we can...

Change is inevitable. Growth is optional.

When we change the way we look at things, the things we look at change.

Change a thought, move a muscle.

Learn to change; change to learn.

Getting sober is easy—just change everything.

Nothing changes if nothing changes.

Insanity is doing the same thing over and over again.

I'm not what I should be. I'm not what I want to be. I'm not what I will be.

I can't change what I don't acknowledge.

Thank God I'm not what I used to be.

Bless them. Change me.

No major changes in the first year.

A door closes and a window has to open.

Nothing will change until you change.

Change is a process and not an event.

Change we must or drink we will.

A door closes, another door opens, and the hallways are a bitch. Don't decorate the hallway.

If I don't change, my sobriety date will.

No one gets better by watching others get well.

Change you must, or drink you will.

Unless you change, your character defects come back wearing different outfits.

If you don't change, you will find yourself on the corner asking for change.

Change or die.

Character Defects

All our character defects are rooted in fear, self-centeredness or selfishness.

You spot it, you got it!

Dating is pouring Miracle Grow on my character defects.

Point a finger and three are pointing back at you.

Don't be a defect in search of a character.

Fear is the mother of all character defects.

Character Defects *continued*

Take care of your character and your reputation will take care of itself.

The monkey's off my back, but the circus is still in town.

"Yea but, yea but," is the mating call for assholes.

My character defects turned out to be assets. I'll never be perfect.

My character defects had become my survival skills. I survived.

Progress not perfection.

When I was drinking, the wake was driving the boat.

I came into AA thinking that I had no defects of character, rather that I was a defective character.

Chip (Coin)

The six-months chip is the "caution chip."

If you want to drink, put your coin under your tongue. When it dissolves, you can drink safely.

Church

See Spirituality.

Courage

Courage is fear that has said its prayers.

Denial

Denial ain't just a river in Egypt.

Push denial out the door, and it'll come back in the window.

Divorce

I lived in a dysfunctional marriage. I got a divorce. I moved and lived alone. I still lived in a dysfunctional family.

Drinking

Nothing is so bad that a drink won't make it worse.

The person takes a drink; the drink takes a drink; the drink takes the person.

Drinking *continued*

My best thinking got me drunk.

Poor me ... poor me ... pour me a drink.

I didn't get in trouble every time I drank, but every time I got in trouble I was drunk.

If you have to control your drinking, it must be out of control.

Anything you did drunk you can do better sober.

The first drink gets you drunk.

If you have to control your drinking, it is already out of control.

Yes, there is relief in drinking. It relieves you of your job, family, home, friends, etc.

The further you are from your last drink, the more expensive your next drink will be.

I only drank on days ending in "y".

If you don't think it's the first drink that gets you drunk, try getting drunk without it.

(The) **Drunk**

A drunk's national anthem: This Time It Will Be Different.

Is the glass half full or half empty? The drunk says it's too small.

A drunk drinks because he wants to. An alcoholic drinks because he has to.

Drunk Dreams

Drunk dreams are gifts from God. They are God's way of reminding us of what it used to be like when we were drinking.

Easy Does It

Easy does it, but do it.

Pain is mandatory; suffering is optional.

When all else fails, follow directions.

Progress not perfection.

Nothing pays off like restraint of tongue or pen.

Expect a Miracle

Sobriety delivers what alcohol promised.

When the student is ready, the teacher will appear.

The joy is in the journey.

Willingness is the key.

Expectation

An expectation is a premeditated resentment.

Great expectations can lead to great disappointments.

Faith

Faith without works is dead.

Courage is faith that has said its prayers.

Wearing my sobriety like a loose garment.

If I leap, the net will appear.

This too shall pass.

Faith is something you don't want in life until you realize that faith is the only thing you have.

Fear

I have a perfect right to be wrong.

Fear is the mother of all character defects.

The worst things I ever lived through never happened.

The itty-bitty-shitty committee in my head is working overtime.

Today is the tomorrow that I worried about yesterday.

You can't change yesterday, but you can ruin today by worrying about tomorrow.

"Overwhelm" is a negative future fantasy.

Fear is not a shortcoming, it's an emotion. Our reaction to it can be a shortcoming.

Fear is a darkroom where negatives are developed.

Fear knocked, faith answered, and no one was there.

When you focus on the problem, it gets bigger. When you focus on the solution, it gets smaller.

I asked God to remove my fear and to help me direct my attention to where it should be.

Feelings

Before sobriety, I couldn't feel and I didn't want to deal.

Feelings aren't facts.

It is strange that once you sober up, you start to feel feelings as they occur rather than having the feelings turn up years later and wondering what these feelings are all about.

You may get upset at the roller coaster feeling, but remember that the roller coaster is always moving ahead.

AA is a do-good program, not a feel-good program.

Feeling good and doing good are not necessarily related.

Don't worry about getting in touch with your feelings. They will get in touch with you.

First Things First

Keep your sobriety first to make it last.

Half measures availed us nothing.

God

See Higher Power

God's Will

We don't always know what God's will is for us, but we always know what it's not.

God could and would if He were sought.

We had to quit playing God.

God has given us so much talent we think we can do it ourselves.

You are exactly where God wants you to be.

Grace

Grace is an unmerited, unwarranted, unearned gift.

The will of God will never take you where the Grace of God will not protect you.

Gratitude

A grateful heart cannot be angry at the same time.

You cannot be grateful and resentful at the same time.

Count your blessings. Write a gratitude list.

Gratitude is a job—not an emotion.

A grateful alcoholic will never drink.

Count your blessings, not your bruises.

Your attitude determines your gratitude.

You can only have one attitude at a time.
So it might as well be one of gratitude.

Guilt

⌒ is the gift that keeps on giving.

⌒ is feeling good about feeling bad.

If you feel guilty for your past, it is guilty by reason of insanity.

Higher Power

I can't handle it, God. You take over.

God will never give you more than you can handle.

God is never late.

When we surrender to our Higher Power, the journey begins.

When I turned myself over to God, I took my life out of the hands of an idiot.

No God ✦ No Peace. Know God ✦ Know Peace.

The results are in God's hands.

Trust God. Clean house. Help others.

Coincidence is a miracle in which God remains anonymous.

There's a God, and it's not you.

If God seems far away, who moved?

There are no atheists in foxholes.

Play it down, pray it up.

Where God guides, God provides.

God cannot do for you what he cannot do through you.

If you want to make God laugh, tell him your plans.

If God brings you to it, he will bring you through it.

God keeps us sober, and AA keeps us asking him/her to keep us sober.

God doesn't have a religion.

The God of our understanding becomes our understanding God.

Can't get a Higher Power? Use the *Group of Drunks*.

Coincidences are God's way of remaining anonymous.

You don't need change or a cell phone to call God.

The spirit of God and the spirits of alcohol don't mix.

God will do for me what I cannot do for myself. But he will not do for me what I can do for myself.

The Higher Power can't be figured out. And if it can be figured out, it is not your Higher Power.

If you could understand God, then he wouldn't be God.

I had a God of my *mis*-understanding.

My Higher Power isn't good or bad.

Hope

I was a hopeless mess. Now I'm a mess with hope.

Hope is faith without knowledge.

Humility

- is the ability to see things as they really are.
- is an honest evaluation of one's good and bad abilities.
- is to be teachable.
- is the ability to accept the help being offered.

"Humility is a perpetual quietness of heart."
(FROM DR. BOB'S DESK PLAQUE)

Being humble isn't that we think less of ourselves. It's that we think of ourselves less.

Humility *continued*

Without anonymity there would be no humility.

Humility is like underwear. It's necessary but it's indecent if it shows.

Humility is our acceptance of ourselves.

Rule 62: Don't take yourself too seriously.

Stay humble so you don't stumble.

True humility is the sincere desire to seek and to do God's will.

If you haven't forgiven yourself for your past behavior, it's due to a lack of humility.

The minute you know you have humility, it is vanity.

Humility is eating crow with a knife and a fork.

Insanity

- is doing the same thing over and over again and expecting a different result.

- is when you go out and drink and know what is going to happen.

Into Action

Don't be a tourist. Swim deep.

Rarely have we seen a person fail who has thoroughly followed our path.

Suit up and show up.

Act as if.

Got to go to any length.

Take the cotton out of your ears and put it in your mouth.

Don't intellectualize. Identify.

Gain self-esteem through esteemable acts.

Half measures availed us nothing.

When all else fails, follow directions.

Utilize, don't analyze.

Don't compare. Identify.

You can't think yourself into right action. You can act yourself into right thinking.

Go to any length.

You got to suit up and show up.

Progress not perfection.

Into Action *continued*

Stick with the winners.

Move a muscle to change a thought.

If you find yourself in a rut, stop digging.

Joy

The joy is in the journey.

Joy is not the absence of sorrow. It is the presence of God.

Just for Today

Going to any length to stay sober.

Keep on trudgin'.

Trust God. Clean House. Help Others.

I can't ✦ He can ✦ I think I'll let him.

Act as if.

Pause when agitated.

Just for today I will try to live through this day only and not tackle all of my life's problems at once.

Let it begin with me.

Be good to yourself.

I have peace of mind in direct proportion to the peace of mind I bring to others.

When you feel left out, reach out.

Growing up so that my experience can benefit others.

There's nothing so bad a drink won't make it worse.

Don't drink even if your ass falls off. If it falls off, put it in a wheelbarrow and take it to a meeting.

Don't believe everything you think.

Today is a very important day. It's the only day you have.

What you do today is important. You're giving up a day of your life for it.

Keep Coming Back

Alcoholism is a progressive disease.

Those who jump in with both feet—succeed.

Keep Coming Back *continued*

I came for my drinking and stayed for my thinking.

A journey of a 1,000 miles begins with the first step.

My best thinking got me the seat in AA.

Keep coming back until you hear your story.

You can act your way into right thinking; you can't think your way into the right action.

You can't stay sober today on yesterday's sobriety.

When I'm alone and thinking, I am behind enemy lines.

Alcoholism is the only disease you can talk yourself out of.

Keep coming back. It works.

Just keep coming.

Keep It Simple

Keep the plug in the jug.

Utilize, don't analyze.

The worst prison is in your own mind.

Just about everything is none of my business.

Just be another bozo on the bus.

Let Go and Let God

If you don't feel close to God, who moved?

If God is your co-pilot, switch seats.

God cannot do for you what he cannot do through you.

God is your employer now.

Our real purpose is to be of maximum service to God and the people around us.

God has given us so much talent we think we can do it ourselves.

We believe in God's goodness more than we believe in our own badness.

Turn it over.

Letting Go

I let go … with claw marks.

If I hang on and don't let go, I'm upside down.

If I don't know, I let it go.

You let go of the past because it's dead.

If the past is blocking your progress, then you are headed in the wrong direction.

Let go or be dragged.

We can best control by letting go.

Life on Life's Terms

No pain, no gain.

Life happens while we're making other plans.

Powerless over people, places and things.

We were entirely ready…

If you believe it, it'll happen.

If you don't believe it, it'll happen anyway.

Please be patient. God isn't finished with me yet.

A door closes, a window has to open, the hallway is a bitch.

It's the willingness to mask the ego.

I have a perfect right to be wrong.

Progress not perfection.

I'm not afraid of dying ... sometimes I'm afraid of living.

Getting better doesn't always feel better.

There are no victims, only volunteers.

That which doesn't kill you serves to make you stronger.

In the end, everything is going to be okay. If it's not okay, it's not the end!

Education is what you get from reading the fine print. Experience is what you get from not reading the fine print.

Good judgment comes from experience, and experience comes from bad judgment.

Life is not a problem to be solved. Life is an adventure to be enjoyed.

Happiness is found along the way, not at the end of the journey.

Just because God opens a door for you doesn't mean he wants you to rush through it.

Live and Let Live

Some of us are sicker than others.

We're only as sick as our secrets.

Patience and tolerance.

Say what you mean, don't say it mean.

Meetings

Go to meetings when you want to and when you don't want to go.

Stand by the coffee pots. It's a good way to meet people.

All you need to start a new meeting are a resentment and a coffee pot.

Don't drink. If your ass falls off, put it in a wheelbarrow and take it to a meeting.

My best thinking got me here.

If hanging around AA doesn't work, try hanging out inside AA.

There are no coincidences in AA.

While we're sitting in this meeting, our disease is doing push-ups in the parking lot.

Take the cotton out of your ears and put it in your mouth.

We're all here because we're not all there.

To keep it, you have to give it away.

A joy shared is twice the joy; a pain shared is half the pain.

Take what you like and leave the rest.

You can't give away what you don't have.

If we don't grow, we gotta go.

Courage to change.

Who you see here ... what you hear here ... when you leave here ... let it stay here.

Utilize. Don't intellectualize.

Analysis ... paralysis.

The time to attend a meeting is when you least feel like going.

Bring the body around and the mind will follow.

Don't compare. Identify.

We go to the meetings for all sorts of reasons, but we don't know what they are, so we keep going to meetings.

Don't compare your insides to someone else's outsides.

Formula for failure: try to please everyone.

An AA meeting is where losers get together to talk about their winnings.

Utilize, don't analyze.

If you want to stay sober, make the coffee.

You have to go to these meetings until you want to.

Become an old-timer ... Don't drink, don't die.

Don't drink ... Don't think ... Go to meetings.

You have to give it away in order to keep it.

If you can't get it done in an hour, you can't get it done.

Drunk School: AA meetings.

You can go to church and hear about miracles, or you can go to a meeting and walk among them.

Okay. So you don't want to do 90 meetings in 90 days. Fine. Don't. Just go to a meeting every day.

We join hands at the end of the meeting to show that we cannot do it alone.

Schedule your day around meetings, not meetings around your day.

Think about your next meeting, not your next drink.

We are forming a circle, not holding hands.

I had to pay the bartender many thousands of dollars to find out that these meetings are free.

When I first came around, I kept listening for the differences in the drinking stories I heard. I kept hearing similarities.

If you think your story is boring, keep it that way.

I can't. We can!

Back Row: Aisle of Denial or Inventory Row.

No one really cares how much you know.
People care how much you care.

In AA meetings I learned not to waste the pain.

Sometimes you need a meeting. Sometimes the meeting needs you.

First I had to learn to listen, and then I listened to learn.

Meeting Makers Make It

People who don't go to meetings don't know what happens to people who don't go to meetings.

The person with the most sobriety at a meeting is the one who got up earliest that morning.

If you start to miss meetings, you will start to miss drinking.

My separation from you keeps me from experiencing the fullness of life.

It's not so much about my showing up for me, but showing up for YOU.

You're only late for your first meeting.

Take the cotton out of your ears and put it in your mouth.

Grow or Go.

God keeps me sober ... meetings are critical.

I show up when I don't want to show up. I ask for help when I don't want to ask for help.

Come to meetings until you want to be here.

I go to a lot of meetings because I never know at which one the miracle will happen, and I want to be there when it does.

Around AA or in AA?

We are not saints.

Some of us go to meetings and continue drinking. Eventually we stop drinking or we stop going to meetings.

I don't come to AA because I can't drink ...
I come to AA because I can drink.

Seven days without an AA meeting makes one weak.

Fake it till you make it.

Keep coming back. It works if you work it. Work it. You're worth it.

The doors swing both ways.

Those who don't go to meetings don't find out what happens to people who don't go to meetings.

Stick with the winners.

Those who criticize don't matter. Those who matter don't criticize.

Most of us don't come to AA meetings on a winning streak.

Willingness always precedes action.

Many meetings, many changes. Few meetings, few changes. No meetings, no changes.

There are only two times I need a meeting. When I feel good and when I feel bad. When I feel good, the meeting needs me. When I feel bad, I need the meeting.

Only one reason not to go to a meeting: a death in the family, and it better be yours.

If you come around long enough, sobriety is just as contagious as alcoholism.

A desire to stop drinking will get you into AA, but it won't keep you there.

Old Timers ✦ New Timers ✦ Some Timers.

Newcomers

Instructions to a newcomer: (1) don't drink under any circumstances, (2) 90 meetings in 90 days, (3) get a sponsor, (4) get a home group, (5) get a Higher Power.

One Day at a Time

If we stay clean just for today, we will never relapse because Every Day is Today.

There are two days in every week over which we have no control: Yesterday and Tomorrow.

If I have one eye on yesterday and one eye on tomorrow, I'll be cockeyed today.

Yesterday is history, tomorrow is a mystery, today is a Gift—that's why they call it the Present.

Yesterday is a cancelled check, tomorrow is a promissory note—only today is cash in the bank.

Today is manageable.

Nothing is going to happen today that you and God can't handle.

Today is the first day of the rest of your life.

If you keep one foot in yesterday and one foot in tomorrow, you're peeing all over today.

Worrying about tomorrow saps today of its strength.

Live every day as if it is your last. Some day you will be right.

One Day at a Time *continued*

I have many 24 hours back to back, but I only have one day.

Stay in the now, not in the never.

You could only get drunk one day at a time. Therefore, you can only stay sober one day at a time.

Don't drink one day at a time. It is important that the one day at a time be consecutive.

Page 449 or Page 417 (in the Big Book)

"And acceptance is the answer to all my problems today. When I am disturbed, it is because I find some person, place, thing, or situation—some fact of my life—unacceptable to me, and I can find no serenity until I accept that person, place, thing, or situation as being exactly the way it is supposed to be at this moment. Nothing, absolutely nothing happens in God's world by mistake. Until I could accept my alcoholism, I could not stay sober; unless I accept life completely on life's terms, I cannot be happy. I need to concentrate not so much on what needs to be changed in the world as on what needs to be changed in me and in my attitudes."

Pain

Pain is the touchstone to spiritual growth.

Pain is the touchstone of progress.

We are only as sick as our secrets.

If you find a path with no obstacles, it probably doesn't lead anywhere.

If you're going through hell, keep going.

The darkest hour is just before the dawn.

Drop the rock.

Problem plus attitude equals two problems.

Pain is mandatory. Suffering is optional.

Nothing I've been through is a mistake.

The darker the hole, the brighter the light.

Don't waste the pain.

People ✦ Places ✦ Things

If you hang around the barbershop long enough, you'll eventually get a haircut.

If you don't want to slip, stay away from slippery places.

People **+** Places **+** Things *continued*

You need to put a lot of people between you and your last drink.

You must change your playmates, play things and play pens.

Perfectionism

Progress, not perfection.

Perfectionism is the highest form of self-abuse.

Perfectionism **+** Procrastination **+** Paralysis.

Powerlessness

People **+** Places **+** Things.

I am powerless over alcohol, and my life is under new management.

I am powerless over anything that makes me feel good for the moment.

Prayer

The pause that refreshes.

Analysis causes paralysis. But prayer will get you there.

Prayer doesn't change God's attitude toward you. Prayer changes your attitude toward God.

If you are praying while you are drinking, that is religion. If you are praying and are not drinking, that's spirituality.

When you pray to God, you don't always get "same day" service.

Prayer and Meditation

If you're too busy to pray, you're too busy.

Be careful what you pray for. You're liable to get it.

If you're too busy to meditate for twenty minutes, then you should meditate for an hour.

Bend your knees before you bend your elbow.

Principles Before Personalities

A friend is a person who can see through you and still enjoy the view.

(The) **Promises** (p. 83-84 in the Big Book)

"If we are painstaking about this phase of our development, we will be amazed before we are half way through.

- 🖋 We are going to know a new freedom and a new happiness.

- 🖋 We will not regret the past nor wish to shut the door on it.

- 🖋 We will comprehend the word serenity and we will know peace.

- 🖋 No matter how far down the scale we have gone, we will see how our experience can benefit others.

- 🖋 That feeling of uselessness and self-pity will disappear.

- 🖋 We will lose interest in selfish things and gain interest in our fellows.

- 🖋 Self-seeking will slip away.

- Our whole attitude and outlook upon life will change.

- Fear of people and of economic insecurity will leave us.

- We will intuitively know how to handle situations which used to baffle us.

- We will suddenly realize that God is doing for us what we could not do for ourselves.

Are these extravagant promises? We think not. They are being fulfilled among us—sometimes quickly, sometimes slowly. They will always materialize if we work for them."

(AA) Recovery

- spiritual literacy.

- spiritual fitness.

- life on life's terms.

- to grow in understanding and effectiveness.

- is a journey out of self.

There is pain in recovery. Misery is optional.

I have an achy heart.

I was going to drink or grow.

The farther I get from my last drunk, the closer I get to my next drunk.

Just another bozo on the bus.

Just another avocado on the conveyor belt.

How do you want to get up the mountain?
Do you want to hike (with AA) or do you want to drive (without AA).

Are you walking toward a drink or away from one?

You can't speed up your recovery, but you can surely slow it down.

Don't drink. Don't think. Don't get married.

The first year you learn how to live without a drink. The second year you learn how to live with yourself. The third year you learn how to live with other people.

At any given moment I am 15 minutes from my past.

Don't compare someone's outsides to your insides.

Came into AA to save my ass and discovered my ass was attached to my soul.

The 4 H's of recovery: If you get Honest, Humble and get Humor, you might get Happiness.

It isn't baggage, garbage or bullshit. It's life.

You can't have everything you want. Where would you put it?

An honest man can only make an honest mistake.

I did not come into AA because I saw the light. I came into AA because I felt the heat.

I'm not responsible for my addiction, but I am responsible for my recovery.

Three months from now you will understand.

I found out that I didn't drink because of my problems. My problems were because I drank.

Live like a camel. Start your day on your knees; end your day on your knees; don't have a drink for 24 hours.

You can make big decisions, but you don't have to make decisions big.

Recovery is a process, not an event.

If you didn't drink today, you had a good day. If you wanted to drink and didn't drink, you had a great day.

Even if you're on the right track, you'll get run over if you just sit there.

If you don't drink, things get good. Then they get real good. Then they get real.

If all I got was sobriety, I would have been shortchanged.

Alcoholism is a progressive disease. Recovery is also progressive.

I stopped asking why and started asking how.

When you get a good idea, get a second opinion.

In early recovery, if it's your idea, don't do it.

Regret

Look back but don't stare.

You can't fix yesterday.

Relapse

Relapse is a process not an event.

No such thing as a relapse. It's a rematch.

Going out is like having sex with a gorilla. It isn't over until the gorilla says it's over.

The AA waltz: Steps 1, 2, 3, out. Steps 1, 2, 3, out.

An alcoholic's way of giving up is to pick up (a drink).

If you go out and drink and don't die, you will want to get back to AA. So don't leave.

Relationships

New in the program? No relationships for one year.

When I first got sober, my sponsor told me that I could have all the sex I wanted in my first year. In the second year, I could have it with other people.

Religion

See Spirituality.

Resentment

The road to resentment is paved with expectation.

A resentment is like taking poison and waiting for the other person to die.

The flip side to forgiveness is resentment.

Resentments are like peeing in your pants; they don't affect anyone quite as much as you.

Today's expectations are tomorrow's resentments.

Serenity

- is being reasonably content most of the time.
- is not the absence of conflict, but the ability to cope with it.

Peace of mind. Peace of heart.

Everything is as it should be.

Serenity Prayer

"God, grant me the serenity to accept the things I cannot change, courage to change the things I can, and the wisdom to know the difference."

—REINHOLD NIEBUHR

"God, grant me the serenity to accept that I am not perfect, the courage to do today what I have to do, and the wisdom to leave the rest of it alone."

Serenity Prayer (Short Forms)

Forget it!

What can't be cured must be endured.

You have to stop crying and start trying.

Service

Coffee makers make it.

Gratitude in action.

To keep it, you have to give it away.

I came to get, and I stayed to give.

Self-Pity

Poor me, poor me, pour me a drink.

There are no victims, only volunteers.

Sharing

Say what you mean but don't say it mean.

If you pass, it's your ass.

Slip

Under every slip is a skirt.

A slip is a premeditated drunk.

If you don't want to slip, stay away from slippery places.

It's not the caboose that kills you, it's the engine.

Seven days without a meeting makes one weak.

What AA gives back to me could take me out again.

I might have another drunk left in me, but do I have another recovery?

The slip occurs before you pick up.

If you fail to change the person you were when you came in, that person will take you out.

Only went out for 30 days and a 1000 nights.

Slips are not a part of the AA program, but they are a part of alcoholism.

Thoroughly have we seen people fail who rarely follow our path.

Picking up a drink is the end of a slip, not the start of it.

AA is the only program where the teacher can become the pupil.

If you don't pick it up, you won't have to put it down.

Slogans

The AA slogans are like railings for the Steps.

Sobriety

A daily reprieve contingent on your spiritual fitness.

It takes time.

Sobriety is incremental.

Sometimes it's "slowbriety."

Willingness is the key.

More will be revealed.

No pain. No gain.

Sobriety *continued*

Keep the plug in the jug.

Pass it on.

My daily sobriety is contingent upon my spiritual condition.

It's the first drink that gets you drunk. It's the last one that gets you sober.

I put down the cork and picked up the fork.

I didn't get sober to be miserable.

Don't quit before the miracle happens.

Early sobriety is like growing up in public.

The longer I'm sober, the drunker I was.

It's a simple journey for confused people with a complicated disease.

When you sober up a horse thief, all you have is a sober horse thief.

You can't keep it unless you give it away.

It's easier to get sober than it is to stay sober.

First we stay sober because we have to. Then we stay sober because we are willing to. Then we stay sober because we want to.

It is easier to stay sober than to try to get sober.

There are three things you must do to stay sober. Don't drink and go to meetings. Don't drink and go to meetings. Don't drink and go to meetings.

When you and I don't take a drink today, we have more in common than all the people I sat and drank with.

A "sober" person has never gone out.

What a sober man has in his heart, a drunken man has on his lips.

From Jail to Yale, from Park Bench to Park Avenue, from Shithouse to Penthouse.

Sobriety begins once you leave the meeting.

Before you can get the gift of sobriety, you have to get the gift of alcoholism.

The first thing you put in front of your sobriety is the second thing you will lose.

Your sobriety has to be more important than anything else, or you will realize you don't have anything else.

Spirituality

Talking about the spiritual part of the AA program is like talking about the wet spot in the ocean.

Religion is for those who fear hell. Spirituality is for those who've been there.

Religion is man made. Spirituality is God given.

Religion wants money. Spirituality doesn't.

Religion demands that you be sinless. Spirituality asks that you sin less.

If you want to save your soul, go to church. If you want to save your ass, go to AA.

A religious person will go to church and think about fishing. A spiritual person will go fishing and think about God.

Listen and don't just hear the noise.

The two most spiritual things you can say in AA are: (1) I don't know, and (2) I need help.

We are spiritual beings having a human experience.

Don't drink, go to meetings, and you will be contacted.

If you pray for a Cadillac and He sends you a jackass—ride it.

There is no competition in the spiritual world. There's enough for everyone.

You don't get into AA by going to church, but you will get into church by going to AA.

Spiritual Awakenings

Spiritual awakenings often come as rude awakenings.

The truth will set you free. But first it'll piss you off.

Sponsor

Sponsor—have one, use one, be one.

To keep it, you have to give it away.

A strong belief in your sponsor is better than a weak belief in a Higher Power.

Call your Sponsor before, not after, you take the first drink.

No human power could have relieved my alcoholism, but my sponsor came damned close.

Sponsor *continued*

If you sponsor yourself you have a fool for a sponsor.

The person who sponsors themselves has a fool for a sponsee.

You want what your sponsor has. He/she has already had what you have.

A good sponsor has bullshit filters in his/her ears.

Steps

The answer is in the Steps.

Life's a dance when you use the Steps.

The elevator is broken, please use the Steps.

Don't wait to get better to do the Steps. Do the Steps now to get better.

The Steps keep us from suicide; the Traditions from homicide.

The first three Steps help us stay sober; the rest help keep us sober.

All the pronouns in the Steps are plural because the Steps are meant to be worked with another—preferably a sponsor.

12 Steps and 12 Traditions

The Steps keep me sober, and the Traditions keep AA alive.

The Steps are spiritual in nature. The Traditions are practical in nature.

The 12 Steps tell us how it works. The 12 Traditions tell us why it works

There are 12 Steps in the ladder of complete sobriety.

The first Step is the only Step a person can work perfectly.

Twelve steps away from a drink...

Steps 1-3: Clear Up ✦ Find a God (Trust God) ✦ Give Up

Steps 4-9: Clean Up ✦ Clean House ✦ Make Up

Steps 10-12: Group Up ✦ Keep Up ✦ Give it Back to Others (Help Others)

Steps 1, 2, 3 (Short Form)

Admit ✦ Commit ✦ Submit

I can't ✦ He can ✦ I think I'll let Him

I came ✦ I came to ✦ I came to believe

Step 1

We admitted we were powerless over alcohol, that our lives had become unmanageable.

There are three parts to Step 1: (1) Admit, (2) Accept, and (3) Do something about it.

"Under the lash of alcoholism, we are driven to A.A., and there we discover the fatal nature of our situation. Then, and only then, do we become as open-minded to conviction and as willing to listen as the dying can be. We stand ready to do anything which will lift the merciless obsession from us." (Twelve Steps and Twelve Traditions, page 24)

Help Me!

We can do what I can't.

You're not alone any more.

None of us come in banging the drums.

Step 2

Came to believe that a Power greater than ourselves could restore us to sanity.

If you do what you always did, you'll get what you always got.

We're here because we're not all there.

Pain was the touchstone to all spiritual growth.

Step 3

Made a decision to turn our will and our lives over to the care of God, as we understood Him.

When you turn your will and your life over to the care of God, your life is none of your business from then on.

Third Step Prayer: Take my will and my life. Guide me in my recovery. Show me how to live.

Let go and let God.

Step 4

Made a searching and fearless moral inventory of ourselves.

Step 4 *continued*

Who you are, where you are, how you got here and where you are going.

"But it is from our twisted relations with family, friends, and society at large that many of us have suffered the most." (TWELVE STEPS AND TWELVE TRADITIONS, PAGE 53)

As an unexamined life is not worth living, the unlived life is not worth examining.

I had to get honest about my dishonesty.

Uncover to recover.

Freedom.

It's okay to look back, but don't stare.

It's okay to visit the past, just don't bring a suitcase.

Do it now or do it when you come back.

If you don't take a 4th, you'll soon pick up a 5th.

Step 5

Admitted to God, to ourselves, and to another human being the exact nature of our wrongs.

Step 6

Were entirely ready to have God remove all these defects of character.

Step 7

Humbly asked Him to remove our shortcomings.

Step 8

Made a list of all persons we had harmed, and became willing to make amends to them all.

"It is the beginning of the end of our isolation from our fellows and from God." (TWELVE STEPS AND TWELVE TRADITIONS, PAGE 82)

Step 9

Made direct amends to such people wherever possible, except when to do so would injure them or others.

Step 10

Continued to take personal inventory and when we were wrong promptly admitted it.

Step 10 *continued*

We shall look for progress, not perfection.

Restraint of tongue and pen.

Step 11

Sought through prayer and meditation to improve our conscious contact with God as we understood Him, praying only for knowledge of His will for us and the power to carry that out.

You cannot stumble when you are on your knees.

Step 12

Having had a spiritual awakening as the result of these steps, we tried to carry this message to alcoholics, and to practice these principles in all our affairs.

Carry the message, not the mess.

Practice these principles in all our affairs ... or change your affairs.

When anyone, anywhere, reaches out for help, I want the hand of AA to be there—and for that, I am responsible.

Be where you are supposed to be; do what you're supposed to do when you're supposed to do it.

The 12 Steps in Plain English

1. Alcohol will kill me.

2. There's a power that wants me to live.

3. Do I want to live or die? (If you want to die, stop here.)

4. Write about how I got to where I am. Tell another person all about me (and let God listen).

5. Want to change.

6. Ask a power greater than myself to help me change.

7. Write down who I've hurt. Fix what I can without hurting anyone else.

8. Accept that I'm human and will screw up.

10. Fix it immediately.

11. Ask a power greater than me to show me how to live.

12. Keep doing 1 through 11 and pass it on.

Surrender

When you find yourself in a hole, stop digging.

We surrender to win, not to whine.

Surrender means being willing to follow someone else's direction.

There is strength in surrender.

Surrender … don't quit.

Think ✦ Think ✦ Think

My first thought is probably wrong. My second is better. And my third thought is probably correct.

Don't believe everything you think.

Whether you think you can or you think you can't, you're right.

This Too Shall Pass

There's nothing so bad that a drink won't make it worse.

If you don't go through the pain, it's wasted.

What will be will be.

There's a way out and a way up.

Nothing happens in God's world by mistake.

Turn It Over

The worst prison is in your own mind.

It's all in God's time.

God is never late.

More will be revealed.

Nothing will happen today that God and I can't handle.

Is it odd … or is it God?

I can't. He can. I think I'll let him.

Give your problems to God … he'll be up all night anyway.

God's plan for me is far greater than my imagination.

God works in mysterious ways.

If God takes you to it … he'll take you through it.

If you do what you always did, you'll get what you always got.

Turn It Over *continued*

Be careful what you pray for...you might get it.

If God seems far away, who moved?

We are not saints.

God is your employer now.

If God is your co-pilot, switch seats.

Prayer—the pause that refreshes.

God cannot do for you what he cannot do through you.

Turn it over!

Worry

In just two days, tomorrow will be yesterday.

There is nothing that heightens the sense of impending doom like impending doom.

And ... Everything Else

We are not human beings having a spiritual experience—we are spiritual beings having a human experience.

If you only quit for one day at a time, every day that you don't drink will be an accomplishment. If you quit forever, you won't have accomplished anything until you're dead.

Rejection is God's protection.

Sick and tired of being sick and tired.

We want what we want when we want it.

Be nice to newcomers ... one day they may be your sponsor.

A defect of character is like a flat tire. A shortcoming is driving on the flat tire.

Depression is anger turned inward.

Wearing life like a lose garment.

Your worth should never depend on another person's opinion.

Keeping right-sized.

The problem with isolating is that you get such bad advice.

Have a good day unless of course you have made other plans.

Serenity is not freedom from the storm but peace amid the storm.

And ... Everything Else *continued*

Wisdom is the ability to see the obvious.

Keep an open mind.

Willingness is the key.

You can't give away what you don't have.

We're responsible for the effort not the outcome.

We don't carry the alcoholic ... we carry the message.

Keep the focus on yourself.

There are no victims, only volunteers.

Life is not a dress rehearsal.

Life is like an onion ... you peel it one layer at a time ... sometimes you cry.

Don't try to teach a pig to sing. Pigs can't sing, and it annoys the pig.

Learn from the mistakes of others. You can't live long enough to make them all yourself.

"No" is a complete sentence.

Wherever you go, there you are.

A dream is a goal with a deadline.

Life is a journey, not a guided tour.

Many times the journey is better than the destination.

When he was drinking he lived like Buck Rogers. Now that he is sober, he lives like Mr. Rogers.

Old-timers used to say that a high bottom drunk hits his own skid row in a white shirt.

What you do today is important, you are giving a day of your life for it.

Life on
Life's Terms

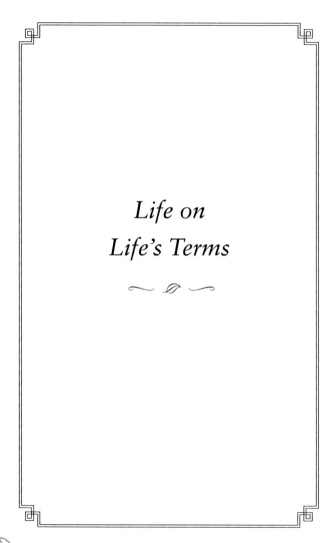

A SPIRITUAL AXIOM

(TWELVE STEPS AND TWELVE TRADITIONS, PAGE 90)

*It is a spiritual axiom
that every time we are disturbed,
no matter what the cause,
there is something wrong with us.
If somebody hurts us and we are sore,
We are in the wrong also.*

THIRD STEP PRAYER

(ALCOHOLICS ANONYMOUS, PAGE 63)

God, I offer myself to Thee—
to build with me and to do
with me as Thou wilt.
Relieve me of the bondage of self,
that I may better do Thy will.
Take away my difficulties,
that victory over them may bear
witness to those I would
help of Thy Power, Thy Love,
and Thy Way of life.
May I do Thy will always.

SEVENTH STEP PRAYER

(*ALCOHOLICS ANONYMOUS, PAGE 76*)

*My Creator, I am now willing
that you should have all of me,
good and bad.
I pray that you now
remove from me every single
defect of character which stands in
the way of my usefulness
to you and my fellows.
Grant me strength, as I go out
from here to do your bidding.
Amen.*

ELEVENTH STEP PRAYER

Prayer of St. Francis of Assisi

(TWELVE STEPS AND TWELVE TRADITIONS, PAGE 99)

Lord, make me a channel of thy peace—

*That where there is hatred,
I may bring love—*

*That where there is wrong,
I may bring the spirit of forgiveness—*

*That where there is discord,
I may bring harmony—*

*That where there is error,
I may bring truth—*

*That where there is doubt,
I may bring faith—*

That where there is despair,
I may bring hope—

That where there are shadows,
I may bring light—

That where there is sadness,
I may bring joy.

Lord, grant that I may seek

Rather to comfort than to be comforted—

To understand, than to be understood—

To love, than to be loved.

for it is by self-forgetting that one finds.

It is by forgiving that one is forgiven.

It is by dying that one awakens
to Eternal Life. Amen.

SERENITY PRAYER

—*REINHOLD NIEBUHR*

*God, grant me the serenity to
accept the things I cannot change,
courage to change the things I can,
and the wisdom to know
the difference.*

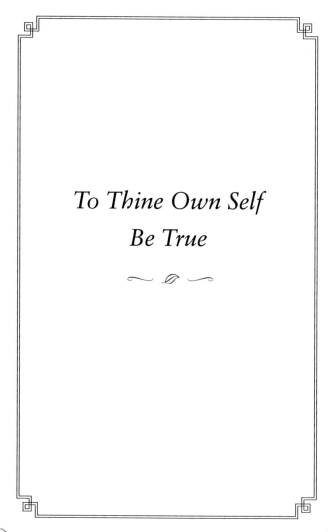

To Thine Own Self Be True

YOU CAN QUICKLY
DIAGNOSE YOURSELF

(ALCOHOLICS ANONYMOUS, PAGE 31)

... We do not like to pronounce any individual as alcoholic, but you can quickly diagnose yourself. Step over to the nearest barroom and try some controlled drinking. Try to drink and stop abruptly. Try it more than once. It will not take long for you to decide, if you are honest with yourself about it. It may be worth a bad case of jitters if you get a full knowledge of your condition.

TWENTY QUESTIONS

Are You an Alcoholic?

This test was prepared by Johns Hopkins University Hospital for use in determining whether or not a person is suffering from alcoholism. Ask yourself the following questions, and answer them as HONESTLY as you can.

1. Do you lose time from work due to drinking?   Yes___No___

2. Is drinking making your home life unhappy?   Yes___No___

3. Do you drink because you are shy with other people?   Yes___No___

4. Is drinking affecting your reputation?   Yes___No___

5. Have you ever felt remorse after drinking?   Yes___No___

6. Have you gotten into financial difficulties as a result of drinking?   Yes___No___

7. Do you turn to lower companions/inferior environments when drinking?   Yes___No___

8. Does your drinking make you careless of your family's welfare?   Yes___No___

9. Has your ambition decreased since you started drinking?   Yes___No___

10 Do you crave a drink at a definite time daily?   Yes___No___

11. Do you want a drink the next morning?   Yes___No___

12. Does drinking cause you to have difficulty in sleeping?   Yes___No___

13. Has your efficiency decreased since you started drinking?   Yes___No___

14. Is drinking jeopardizing your job or business?   Yes___No___

15. Do you drink to escape from worries or trouble?   Yes___No___

16. Do you drink alone?   Yes___No___

17. Have you ever had a loss of memory (blackout) as a result of drinking?   Yes___No___

18. Has your physician ever treated
you for drinking? Yes___No___

19. Do you drink to build up your
self-confidence? Yes___No___

20. Have you ever been to a hospital
or institution on account of
drinking? Yes___No___

If you have answered YES to any *one* of the questions, that is a definite warning that you MAY be an alcoholic.

If you have answered YES to any *two*, CHANCES ARE that you are an alcoholic.

If you have answered YES to *three or more*, YOU ARE DEFINITELY AN ALCOHOLIC.

ALCOHOL SCREENING FOR TEENS

—DEVELOPED BY JOHN KNIGHT, MD

1. Have you ever ridden in a car driven by someone (including yourself) who was "high" or had been using alcohol or drugs?

2. Do you ever use alcohol or drugs to relax, feel better about yourself or fit in?

3. Do you ever forget things you did while using alcohol or alone?

4. Do your family or friends ever tell you that you should cut down on your drinking or drug use?

5. Have you ever gotten into trouble while you were using alcohol or drugs?

If you have answered Yes to two or more questions, we recommend that you speak with someone to see if alcohol or drugs are a problem for you and to get help.

Don't Quit
Five Minutes Before
the Miracle Happens

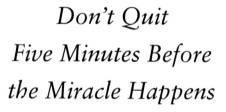

REFERENCES

Alcoholics Anonymous World Services, Inc., *Alcoholics Anonymous*, 3rd edition, New York City, 1976. (Also known as the *Big Book of AA*)

Alcoholics Anonymous World Services, Inc., *Twelve Steps and Twelve Traditions*, New York, 1952.

Carr, D., "Me and My Girls," the *New York Times* Magazine, July 20, 2008, p. 50.

J. R. Knight, L. A. Shrier, T. D. Bravender, M. Farrell, J. Vanderbilt, H. H. Shaffer, "A new brief screen for adolescent substance abuse," Archives of Pediatric and Adolescent Medicine [1999]: 153; 591-596.

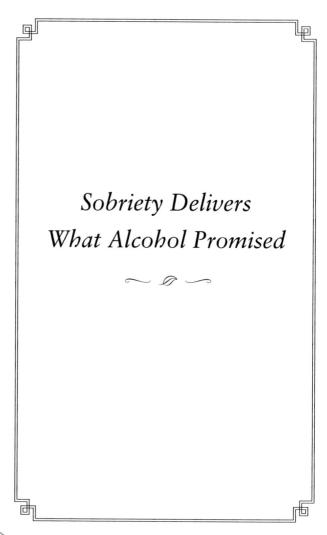

Sobriety Delivers
What Alcohol Promised

HERE'S WHAT I HEARD IN AA